Capstone Short Biographies

Women in Computer Science Careers

by Jetty Kahn

Consultant:
Kathy A. Tomlinson, Ph.D.
Associate Professor of Mathematics
University of Wisconsin, River Falls

CAPSTONE BOOKS
an imprint of Capstone Press
Mankato, Minnesota

Capstone Books are published by Capstone Press
818 North Willow Street, Mankato, MN 56001
http://www.capstone-press.com

Library of Congress Cataloging-in-Publication Data
Kahn, Jetty.
    Women in computer science careers/by Jetty Kahn.
    p. cm.—(Capstone short biographies)
    Includes bibliographical references and index.
    Summary: Describes the careers of five women working in the computer
science field: Maria Gini, Jessica Hodgins, Fern Hunt, Bonnie Labosky, and
Misha Mahowald.
    ISBN 0-7368-0316-5
    1. Computer science—Vocational guidance—Juvenile literature. 2. Computers
and women—Juvenile literature. [1. Computer scientists. 2. Woman Biography.]
I. Title. II. Series.
QA76.25.K35 2000
004'.092'2—dc21
[B]   99-14450
                                                                            CIP

Editorial Credits
Connie R. Colwell, editor; Timothy Halldin, cover designer; Kia Bielke, illustrator;
    Heidi Schoof, photo researcher

Photo Credits
Bonnie Labosky, 32, 35
Fern Hunt, 26
Georgia Tech Animation Laboratory, 22, 25
International Stock/Jay Thomas, 6; Chad Ehlers, 30; Wayne Aldridge, 36
Jessica Hodgins, 18
Misha Mahowald, 9, 38
Patrick O'Leary, cover, 12
Photo Network, 4; Lonnie Duka, 16; 21
Shaffer Photography/James L. Shaffer, 43
Unicorn/Travis Evans, 15; Joseph Sohm/Chromosohm, 29
University of Minnesota, 10

Table of Contents

Chapter 1

Computer Science

Computer science is the study of computers and how they work. Computer scientists design computers and the programs that run them. Computer scientists use computers to explore questions and solve problems in many areas. Science, health, entertainment, and other areas benefit from the work of computer scientists.

Computer scientists can work in different settings. Some computer scientists work at schools, colleges, or universities. Others work for companies or businesses.

Computer science is the study of computers and how they work.

People who enjoy using computers to find answers to problems may make good computer scientists.

Computer Science Specialties

Computer scientists can specialize in many different fields. Some computer scientists work in the education field. These scientists often teach at schools, colleges, or universities. Many also do research. Research is the study of a subject. Scientists do research by reading and conducting experiments. Computer scientists usually research subjects related to computer science.

Some computer scientists work in the medical field. These scientists may use computers to design medicines or medical machines. They may use computers to find and identify illnesses. Some even use computers to track the spread of diseases.

Computer scientists may work in other areas. Some study the weather or changes in the earth. These scientists make computer images of land, air, or water patterns. The images help them forecast changes in the earth such as volcanoes, earthquakes, and floods. Some computer scientists work in the entertainment industry. These scientists produce pictures on computers. The pictures often are used in magazines, television, and movies.

Education

People who like to solve challenging problems often make good computer scientists. These people may enjoy using computers to find answers to problems. They may like to come up with new and creative ways to perform tasks.

People who want to be computer scientists must attend a college or university. As students, they take classes in mathematics, science, and computers. They may earn a bachelor's degree in computer science or a related area. Students usually earn this degree in four years at a college or university. Some computer scientists find jobs after earning a bachelor's degree. These computer scientists may teach elementary or high school classes. They may design products for businesses. They also may use their computer skills in other areas of work.

Many computer scientists later go on to earn a master's or doctoral degree. Doctoral degrees are the most advanced degrees offered by universities. Computer scientists with doctoral degrees may teach in colleges or universities. Many also may do research for companies that need these highly trained computer specialists.

Not all computer scientists have degrees in computer science. Many of these scientists study other subjects. Degrees in mathematics, chemistry, or other sciences also can lead to careers in computer science. Computer scientists can apply their knowledge in other fields to computer science.

People who want to be computer scientists must earn a college degree.

Chapter 2

Maria Gini

As a computer scientist, Maria Gini builds cars from toy blocks. Gini uses computers to control these cars. She hopes to learn more about how to control these cars by performing experiments.

Gini was born in Milan, Italy. She earned a doctoral degree in physics from the University of Milan. Scientists in physics study matter and energy. Physicists often study the way things move from place to place. Today, Gini teaches computer science at the University of Minnesota in Minneapolis.

Maria Gini teaches computer science at the University of Minnesota in Minneapolis.

Maria Gini's robot car has light sensors to detect a lightbulb.

Robot Cars

Gini designs robots and controls them by computer. Robots are machines that can be programmed to perform tasks that people usually perform.

One of Gini's robots is a toy car with a trailer. The robot car has sensors. These instruments detect changes in the car's surroundings. Sensors can detect changes in heat, light, pressure, or sound. The car's sensors send information about these changes back to a computer. The computer then uses this information to tell the robot car what to do next.

Gini may want the car to back the trailer into a small parking space. Gini provides the robot car with light sensors. She places a small lightbulb in the parking spot. The car's light sensors can detect the bulb. Gini uses the computer to tell the robot to go toward the lightbulb.

The robot car does not back up correctly the first several times. Gini uses the computer to give the car new commands each time it makes a mistake. For example, the computer tells the car to go to the right if it turns too far to the left. The car finally backs up correctly.

Gini programs other robots to do more difficult tasks. She programs robots to move through rooms without bumping into objects. To do this, Gini gives these robots light or sonar sensors. Sonar sensors detect changes in sound instead of light.

Gini even programs robots to avoid other moving objects. Robots programmed this way use their sonar sensors to detect the movements of the objects around them. The sensors help the robots know in which direction to move to avoid the objects.

Sensor Research

People also have sensors. People's ears and hands have sensors. People listen to detect changes in their surroundings. People can use their hands to feel their surroundings.

Animals also have sensors. Dolphins, whales, and bats send out sonar waves. These waves bounce off objects around the animals. The waves then bounce back to the animals to help them sense the objects. Bats can sense insects as small as mosquitoes up to 18 feet (5 meters) away.

Computer scientists study human and animal sensors. They want to use knowledge about sensors to learn how to make better robot sensors. Robots with better sensors someday may help people with many tasks.

Trial and Error

People learn by trial and error. For example, some beginning divers try to perform a certain

Whales use sonar sensors to sense the objects around them.

Beginning divers learn to perform dives by trial and error.

dive. They may fail several times before they learn to perform the dive correctly.

Gini programs robots to operate by trial and error. The robots try different ways of doing a task until they find the way that works best. For example, a robot car usually tries 20 or 30 times before it parks its trailer correctly. But the robot car then can park correctly each time. It only needs to be in range of the lightbulb.

Robot Uses

Robots that operate by trial and error perform their tasks correctly each time once they learn them. These robots then do not need people to operate them.

Robots that operate by trial and error can be programmed to help people with many tasks. They may help blind people find objects at home. They may take museum visitors through exhibits. Robots may help people find information desks at airports or books in libraries. Robots may gather rock samples in outer space. They may take photographs deep under the sea. Robots even may help bring food to sick people.

Robots that assist people still have some problems. Most robots cannot climb stairs. They can get lost using elevators. Robots also are expensive. Gini and other computer scientists are working to improve robots. They hope robots someday may help people with many complex tasks.

Chapter 3

Jessica Hodgins

Jessica Hodgins enjoys flying stunt kites. People move the strings of these kites to make them dive and turn. Hodgins flies stunt kites for fun. But she also knows a great deal about the way objects such as stunt kites move. As a computer scientist, Hodgins uses computers to make realistic pictures of moving objects.

Hodgins studied computer science at the Massachusetts Institute of Technology (MIT). She then earned a doctoral degree in computer science at Carnegie Mellon University (CMU) in Pittsburgh, Pennsylvania.

Jessica Hodgins uses computers to create realistic images of moving objects.

Today, Hodgins is a professor at the College of Computing at the Georgia Institute of Technology. She studies movement by building robots and creating computer images.

Movement Research

People change weight from one leg to the other as they run. One leg balances the body as the other gets ready for the next step.

At CMU, Hodgins built a robot that also changed its weight from leg to leg. This allowed the robot to run like a person. The robot jumped over objects, climbed stairs, and did flips.

Hodgins also created computer animations of robots' movements. These drawings are shown quickly one after the other on the computer screen. This makes the objects in the drawings appear to move. The computer animations helped Hodgins create robots that moved like people.

People change weight from one leg to the other when they run.

Computer Simulations

Today, Hodgins uses computers to create animations of athletes. These pictures are called computer simulations. Hodgins makes simulations of runners, bikers, divers, and gymnasts.

Hodgins uses mathematics and computer programs to simulate the movements of athletes on the computer. Athletes can learn ways to improve their performances by watching these computer simulations. For example, Hodgins can make simulations of divers. The images may show divers what mistakes they make each time they dive. Divers can learn ways to improve their diving skills when they watch the computer simulations.

Hodgins must understand people's bodies in order to make realistic simulations. Hodgins must know how the body's limbs, joints, and muscles work. She must understand how these parts fit together. Only realistic simulations can help athletes improve their performances.

Jessica Hodgins makes computer simulations of athletes to help them improve their performances.

Hodgins also must know about the sports in which these athletes compete. For example, Hodgins must know how gymnasts' bodies appear during certain moves. She must know how bicyclists' legs move while they pedal. This knowledge helps Hodgins create realistic images for each sport.

Simulation Research

In the future, Hodgins hopes to make computer simulations of shopping malls and offices. This may help architects design better buildings. Architects may examine the simulations to learn the best locations for elevators and stairs. Office simulations may help employees learn the best ways to sit, stand, and move while they work. This may help prevent injuries at workplaces.

Today, scientists must give computers instructions to create simulations. Hodgins

Jessica Hodgins must know how gymnasts' bodies move to create realistic computer simulations.

hopes to create robots and computers that can make simulations on their own. Scientists then could send computers to outer space and other places too dangerous for people. The computers could make simulations of these places for scientists to study.

Chapter 4

Fern Hunt

People want products that look good and last a long time. Many products have surfaces to protect them. Fern Hunt uses computers to make models of these surfaces. She then studies these models to learn how to improve these surfaces in the future.

Hunt studied mathematics to prepare for a career as a computer scientist. She earned a bachelor's degree from Bryn Mawr College in Bryn Mawr, Pennsylvania. She earned a doctoral degree in mathematics from New York University in the city of New York.

Fern Hunt uses computer science to study the materials people use in their everyday lives.

Today, Hunt works at the National Institute of Standards and Technology in Gaithersburg, Maryland. She uses her skills in computer science to study materials people use in their everyday lives.

Surfaces

Most products have surfaces that help protect them. For example, cars have hard metal shells to protect their engines and other parts. Countertops have hard plastic surfaces to protect them from things such as knives.

Surface materials can be paint, plastic, or even magnets. Credit cards and computer disks have magnetic surfaces. Computers can read information from these magnets.

Every surface consists of hundreds of microscopic parts. People must look through a microscope to see such small parts. These parts sometimes lose their form or wear down over time. For example, glossy paint can fade from wear. The magnets on credit cards can be damaged from use.

Cars have hard metal shells to protect their engines and other parts.

Computer Models

Hunt makes computer models of protective surface parts. She uses the models to test these surfaces on computer screens. The computer models show whether the surfaces will crack or fade over time.

Hunt then makes predictions about the microscopic parts of these surfaces. Predictions are educated guesses about what

will happen. She studies the parts of glossy paint. She predicts how weather and other factors will affect these parts. Hunt studies the magnets on credit cards. She predicts how heat or light will damage the magnets' parts.

Hunt's predictions help companies make better products. Companies use Hunt's information when they make surfaces to protect their products. The companies then can make stronger and longer-lasting surfaces for their products.

Companies use Fern Hunt's predictions to make better surfaces for their products.

Chapter 5

Bonnie Labosky

As a young girl, Bonnie Labosky enjoyed solving math problems with her father. Today, Labosky uses her skills in mathematics and computer science to design computer programs. These programs help people with heart problems.

Labosky studied mathematics to prepare for her career in computer science. She earned a bachelor's degree in mathematics at Mercyhurst College in Pennsylvania. She earned a master's degree at the University of Notre Dame in South Bend, Indiana. She then

Bonnie Labosky designs computer programs to help people with heart problems.

earned a doctoral degree in computer science from the University of Minnesota.

Software

Labosky began working for a company in Minnesota that sold computer programs. Labosky designed computer software at the company. Software controls computers and instructs them to perform specific tasks. Labosky designed software for large businesses such as banks.

Labosky also created software for people to use in their homes and offices. These programs helped people learn how to use their computers. Many of these software programs were fun and easy to use. Some of the programs even showed colorful pictures on the computer screens.

The software company became very successful. It sold many computer programs. The company decided to move its offices to Chicago due to its success.

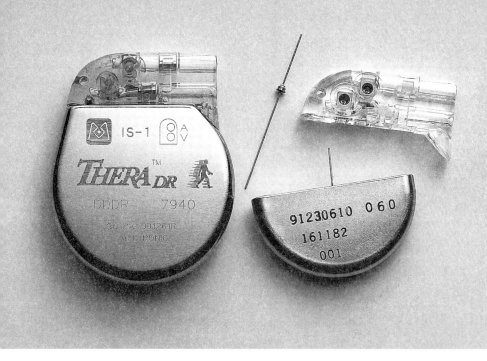

Bonnie Labosky makes software programs to control electronic medical devices such as cardiac pacemakers.

Electronic Medical Devices

Labosky and her family did not want to leave Minnesota. Labosky began designing computer software for a medical manufacturer in Minneapolis. This company is called Medtronic. This company makes electronic medical devices that are placed inside people's bodies. Some of these devices control pain. Others help damaged muscles and nerves. For

example, cardiac pacemakers help people with weak hearts.

Labosky's software makes the electronic medical devices work properly. The software reports when the batteries in the devices need to be replaced. Doctors then operate on the patients to replace the batteries. The software programs also instruct people's hearts to beat faster when the people exercise.

Labosky's software programs help patients and doctors. Labosky's software allows doctors to make quicker and better decisions about their patients. The software helps patients get the treatment they need.

Today, Labosky manages 500 people at Medtronic. Many are scientists who work to create new or better electronic medical devices. Labosky often helps workers at Medtronic decide which new products they should make.

Software controls computers and instructs them to perform specific tasks.

Chapter 6

Misha Mahowald

As a child, Misha Mahowald enjoyed watching her favorite television program. She wondered how people see the objects on television and around them. Mahowald wanted to learn how the brain helps people see.

Mahowald studied both computers and the science of living things. She earned a bachelor's degree in biology at the California Institute of Technology (CIT). Scientists in this field study the parts of living things. She then earned a doctoral degree in computational neuroscience at CIT. Neuroscience combines biology and computer science to try to understand the brain.

Misha Mahowald wanted to understand how the brain works to make people see.

The Eye

People's eyes and brains work together to allow people to see the objects around them. Objects reflect light. The light from these objects enters a hole in the middle of the eye called the pupil. A lens behind the pupil then directs the light to the back of the eye. The lens focuses the light at a lining of special cells called the retina. The light on the retina forms an upside-down image. The retina then sends messages about this image to the brain.

These messages travel along special cells to the visual cortex of the brain. The visual cortex understands the messages. This process allows people to see the objects around them.

Computers usually process information millions of times faster than the human brain. But computers do not see like people do. They do not have retinas to help change light into images. Computers cannot see colors, movement, or shapes in the way that

The Parts of the Eye

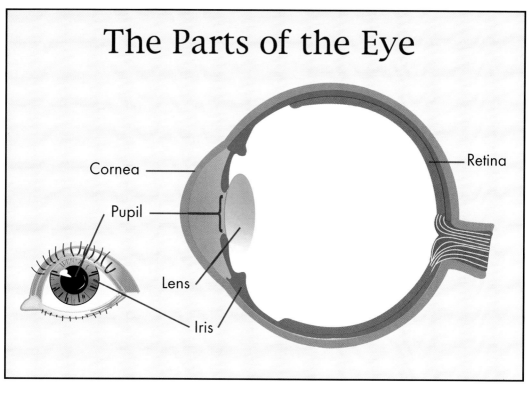

Cornea

Pupil

Lens

Iris

Retina

people can. Computers also have trouble understanding images. Computers easily can recognize shapes. But they have difficulty identifying objects. For example, a computer knows a peach is round. But it does not know it is a peach.

Mahowald wanted to design computers that understand images in the way people understand them. She studied human eyes and brains. She wanted to learn how to make a computer that could see like a person.

Silicon Retinas

Mahowald built a model of the retina. She built the model from tiny electrical parts made of silicon. This element is found in sand and rocks. She put the silicon retina inside a computer.

The computer with the silicon retina operated much like human sight. This computer could identify an image. The computer's electrical signals began to fire when it saw Mahowald's face. This is the same way people's brains react when people see a person or object they recognize. The computer recognized the shape and identity of Mahowald's face.

Silicon Retinas in the Future

Today, robots use sensors to move. But robots can get lost using sensors. In the future, silicon retinas may help robots see as humans see. These robots then could help people with many tasks.

Silicon retinas someday may help blind people see.

Silicon retinas also may help blind people. Doctors someday may operate to replace damaged retinas with silicon retinas.

Mahowald made important discoveries that linked biology and computer science. She died in 1996 at the age of 33. But scientists like Mahowald continue to find ways to bring these sciences together.

Words to Know

animation (an-i-MAY-shuhn)—a series of drawings projected quickly so that the characters in the drawings seem to move

lens (LENZ)—the clear part of the eye that focuses light on the retina

microscopic (mye-kruh-SKOP-ik)—too small to be seen without a microscope

pupil (PYOO-puhl)—the round, black part of the eye that lets light travel through the eye

retina (RET-uhn-uh)—the area at the back of the eye that sends signals to the brain

sensor (SEN-sur)—an instrument that can detect changes in heat, light, pressure, or sound; sensors send this information to a controlling device such as a computer.

software (SAWFT-wair)—computer programs that control the workings of computers and direct them to perform specific tasks

To Learn More

Flansburg, Scott. *Math Magic for Your Kids: Hundreds of Games and Exercises from the Human Calculator to Make Math Fun and Easy.* New York: HarperPerennial, 1998.

Kahn, Jetty. *Women in Engineering Careers.* Capstone Short Biographies. Mankato, Minn.: Capstone High/Low Books, 1999.

Perl, Teri. *Women and Numbers: Lives of Women Mathematicians plus Discovery Activities.* San Carlos, Calif.: Wide World Publishing/Tetra, 1993.

Taylor, Kim. *Structure.* Flying Start Science. New York: J. Wiley, 1992.

Useful Addresses

Association for Women in Computing
P.O. Box 5781
Bethesda, MD 20824-5781

Association for Women in Mathematics
4114 Computer & Space Sciences Building
University of Maryland
College Park, MD 20742

Association for Women in Science
1200 New York Avenue NW
Suite 650
Washington, DC 20005

Society for Canadian Women in Science and Technology
417-535 Hornby Street
Vancouver, BC V6C 2E8
Canada

Internet Sites

Bats4Kids
http://members.aol.com/bats4kids

**BLS Career Information: Computer
  Scientist**
http://www.bls.gov/k12/html/mat_005.htm

How Computer Programs Work
http://www.howstuffworks.com/program.htm

Kids' Camps
http://www.kidscamps.com

MIT Leg Lab: On the Run
http://www.ai.mit.edu/projects/leglab/
  simulations/otr/otr.html

The Robot Zoo
http://www.sgi.com/robotzoo

Index